jazz fusion

Arranged by Brent Edstrom

contents

title		artist
2	AFFIRMATION	GEORGE BENSON
6	CAPTAIN FINGERS	LEE RITENOUR
10	CHAMELEON	HERBIE HANCOCK
14	THE CHICKEN	JACO PASTORIUS
18	CONTUSION	STEVIE WONDER
21	CHROMOZONE	MIKE STERN
26	DON'T STOP	JEFF LORBER
30	FEELS SO GOOD	CHUCK MANGIONE
34	500 MILES HIGH	RETURN TO FOREVER
38	GOODBYE PORK PIE HAT	CHARLES MINGUS
46	GOT A MATCH?	CHICK COREA
41	MEETING OF THE SPIRITS	MAHAVISHNU ORCHESTRA
50	MERCY, MERCY, MERCY	JOE ZAWINUL
54	MILE HIGH	YELLOWJACKETS
62	OOPS	STEPS AHEAD
66	PEACHES EN REGALIA	FRANK ZAPPA
70	PORTRAIT OF TRACY	JACO PASTORIUS
72	RED BARON	BILLY COBHAM
76	RED CLAY	FREDDIE HUBBARD
80	A REMARK YOU MADE	WEATHER REPORT
59	SNAKES	BOB BERG/DAVID SANBORN
84	THING OF GOLD	SNARKY PUPPY
88	WINELIGHT	GROVER WASHINGTON JR.
94	YOU KNOW WHAT I MEAN	JEFF BECK

ISBN 978-1-5400-1544-0

Visit Hal Leonard Online at
www.halleonard.com

Contact Us:
Hal Leonard
7777 West Bluemound Road
Milwaukee, WI 53213
Email: info@halleonard.com

In Europe contact:
Hal Leonard Europe Limited
42 Wigmore Street
Marylebone, London, W1U 2RN
Email: info@halleonardeurope.com

In Australia contact:
Hal Leonard Australia Pty. Ltd.
4 Lentara Court
Cheltenham, Victoria, 3192 Australia
Email: info@halleonard.com.au

AFFIRMATION

By JOSÉ FELICIANO

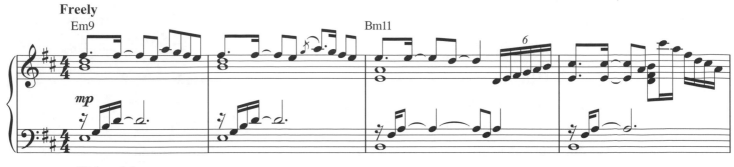

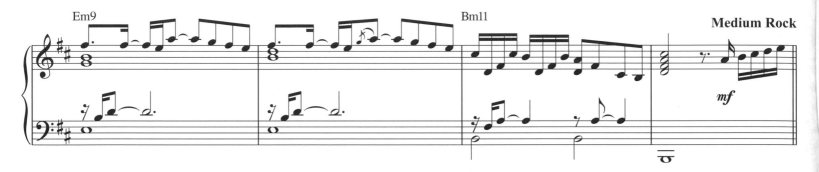

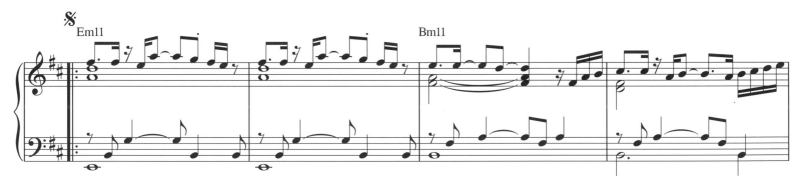

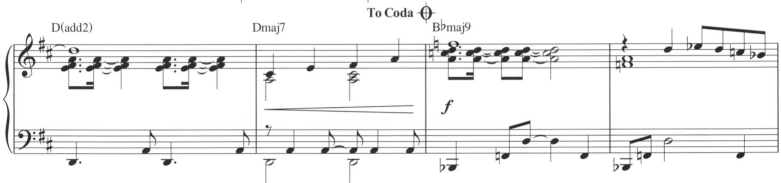

To Coda

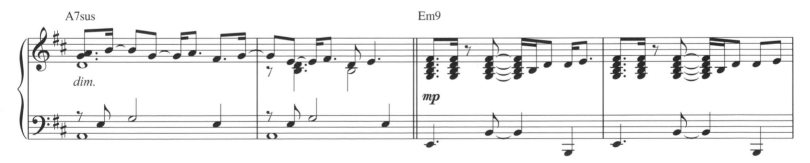

4

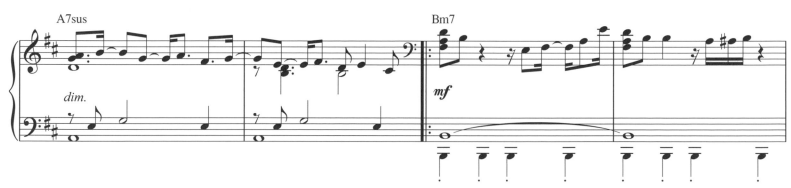

CAPTAIN FINGERS

By LEE RITENOUR

Moderately

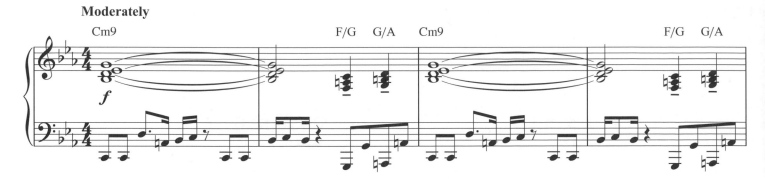

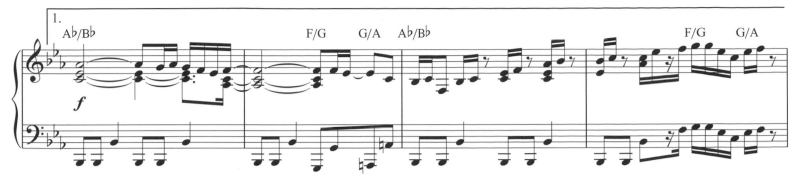

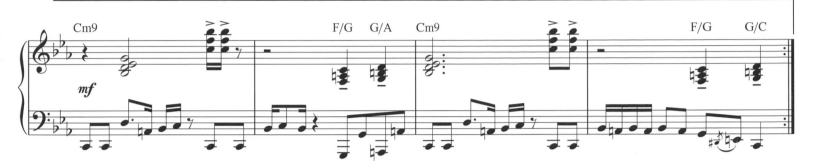

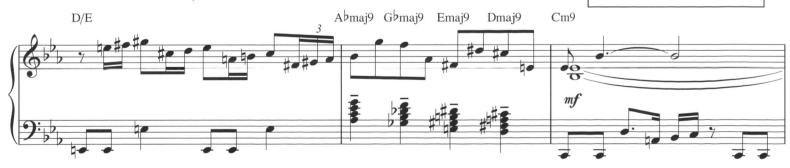

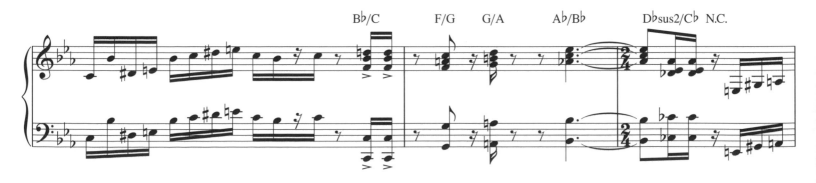

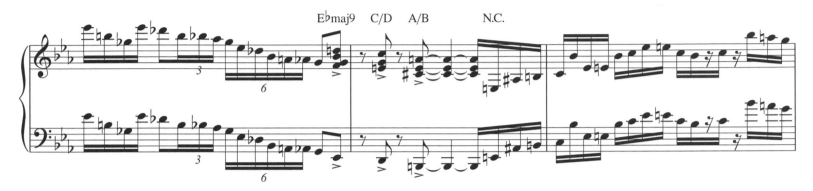

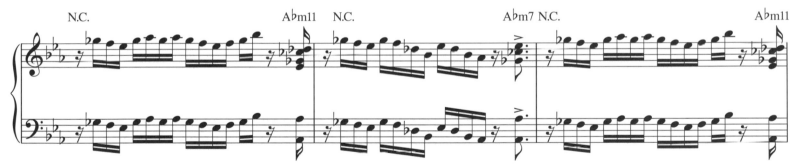

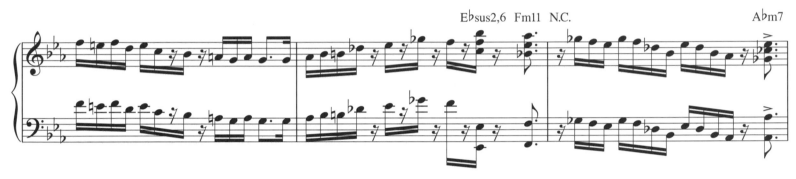

CHAMELEON

By HERBIE HANCOCK,
PAUL JACKSON, HARVEY MASON
and BENNIE MAUPIN

Medium

To Coda ⊕
Play 3 times

Play 3 times

12

Swing 16ths

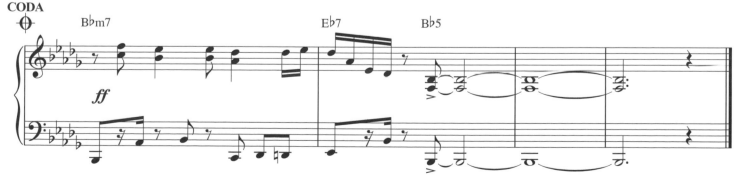

THE CHICKEN

By ALFRED ELLIS

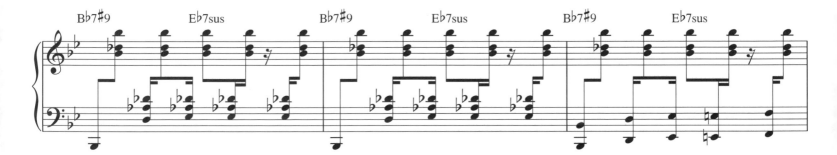

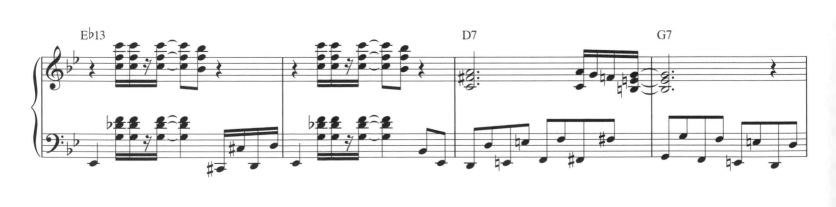

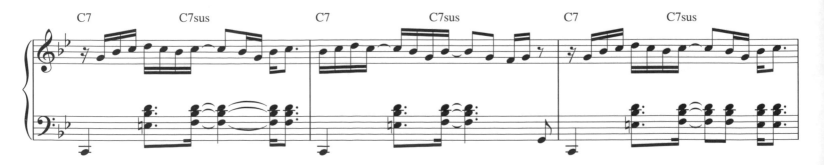

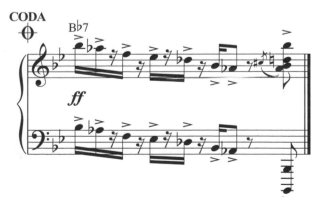

CONTUSION

Words and Music by
STEVIE WONDER

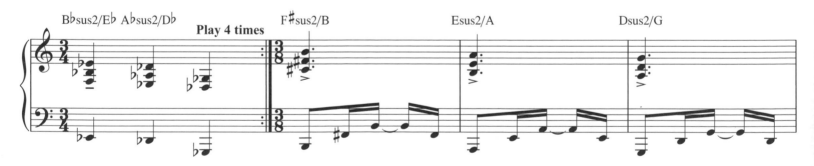

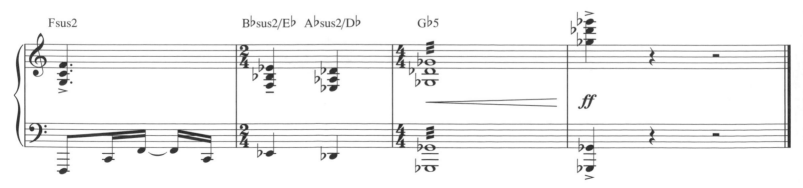

CHROMOZONE

By MIKE STERN

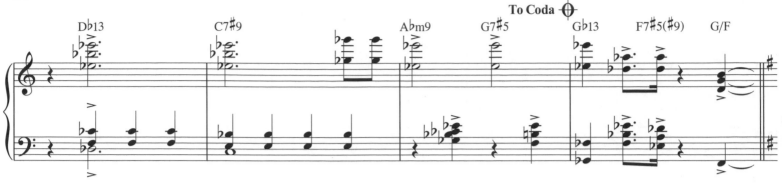

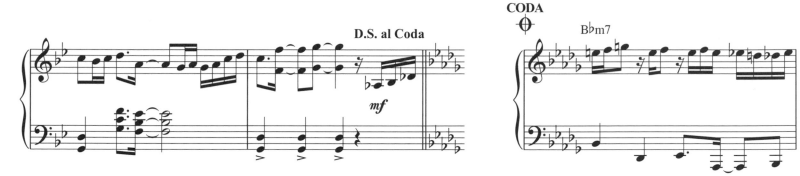

DON'T STOP

By JEFF LORBER
and REX RIDEOUT

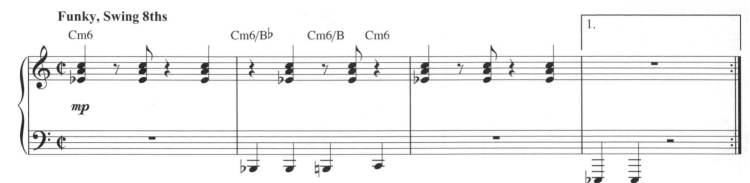

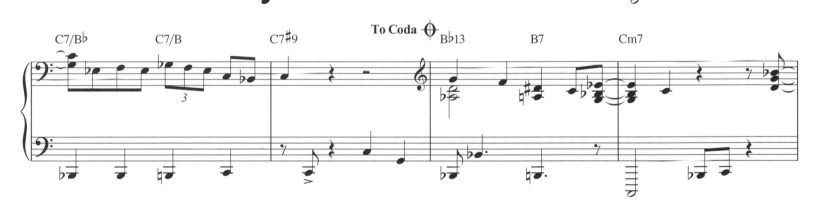

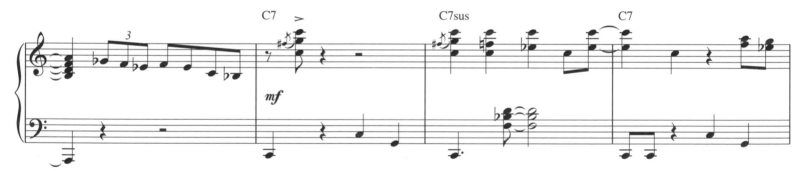

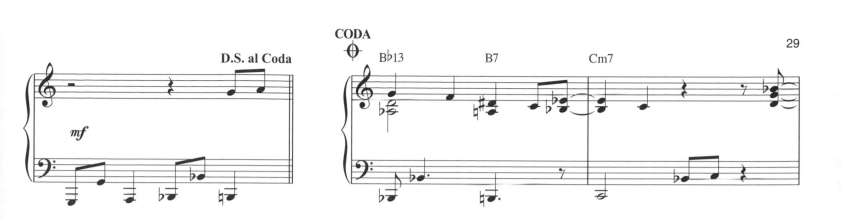

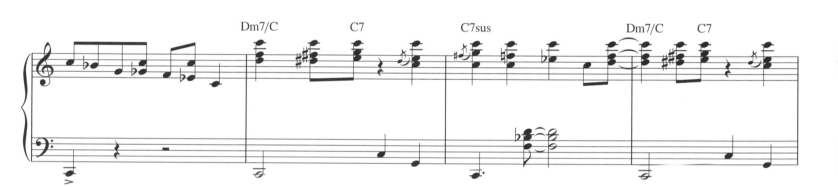

FEELS SO GOOD

By CHUCK MANGIONE

Freely, with rubato

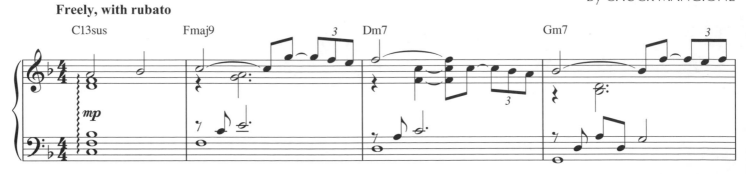

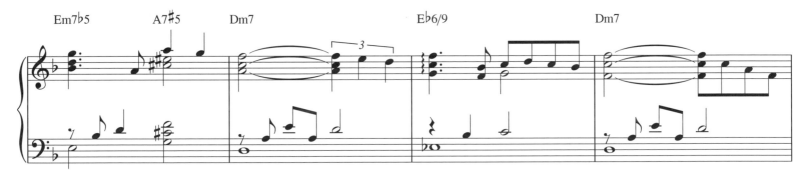

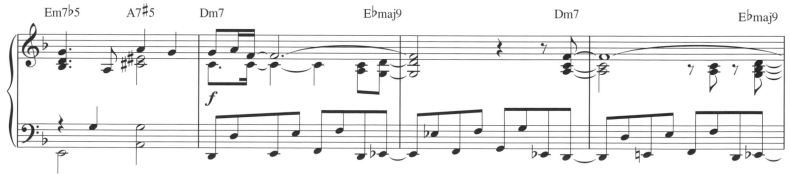

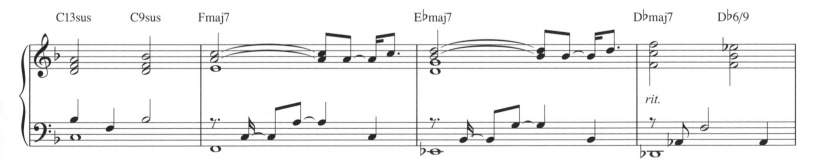

500 MILES HIGH

Words by NEVILLE POTTER
Music by CHICK COREA

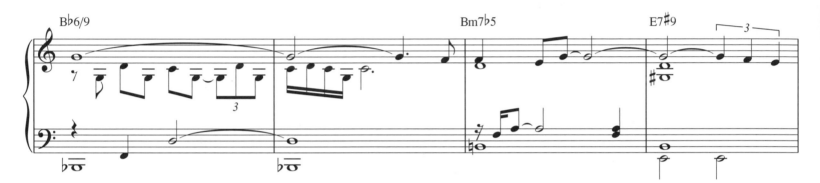

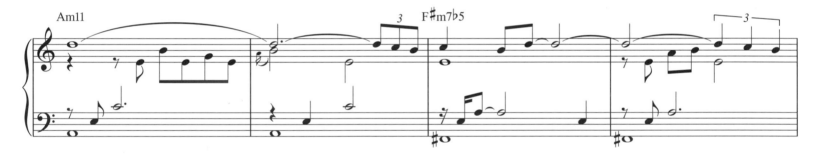

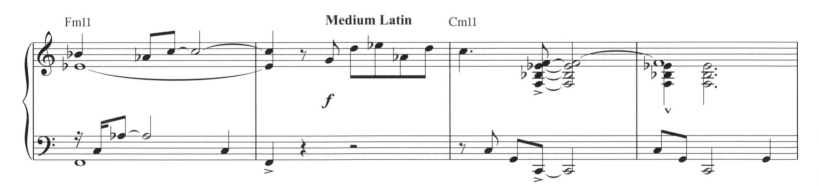

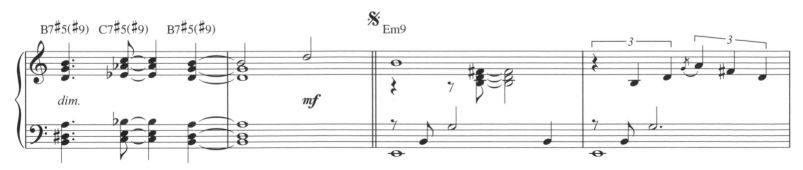

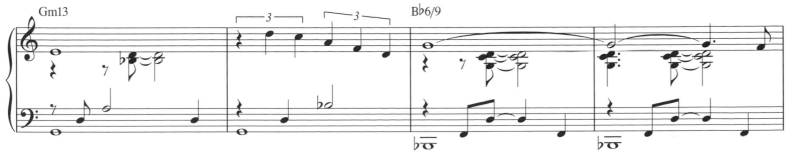

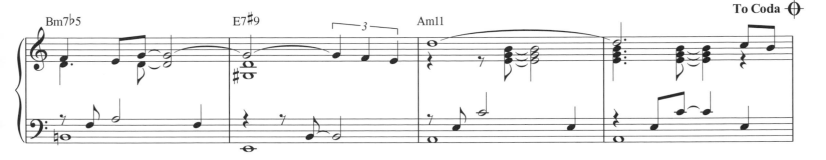

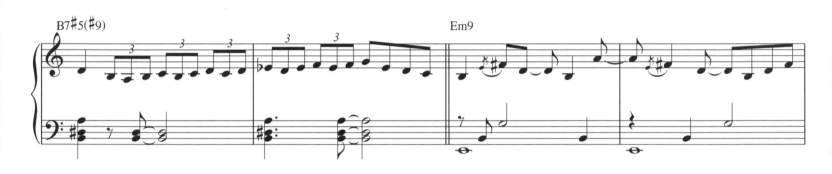

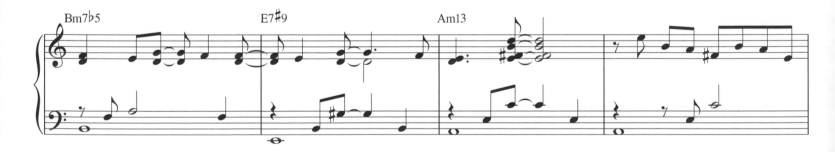

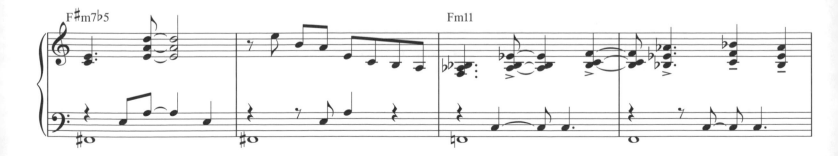

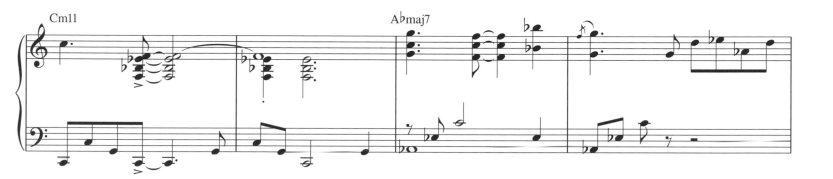

GOODBYE PORK PIE HAT

By CHARLES MINGUS

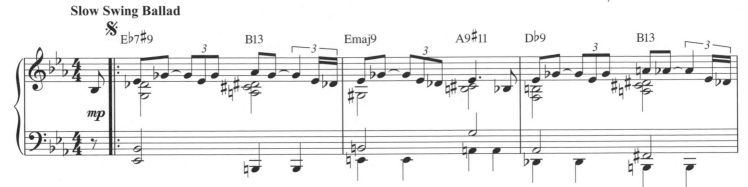

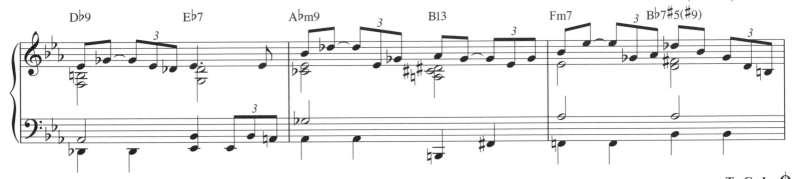

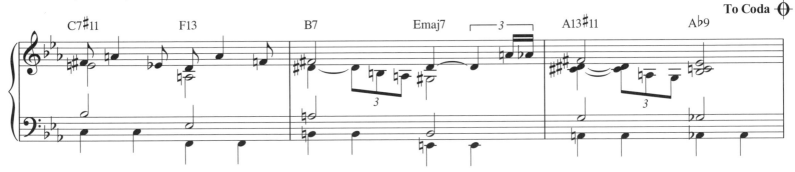

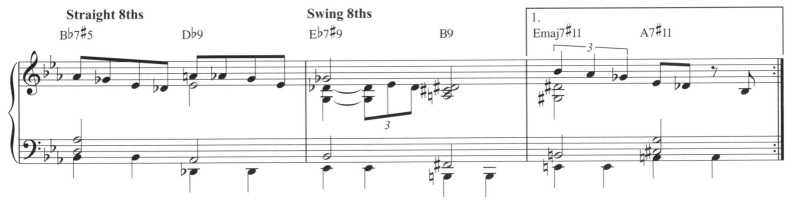

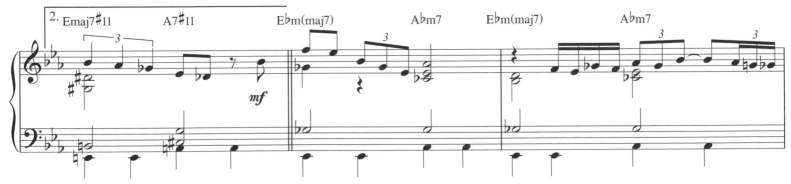

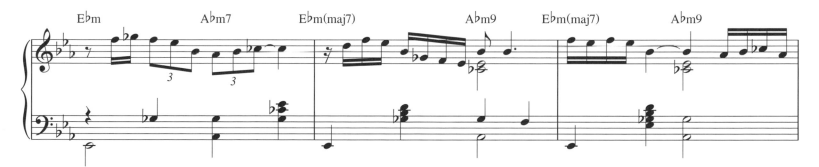

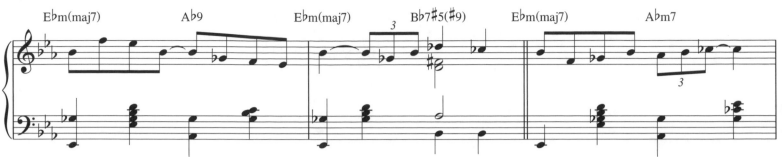

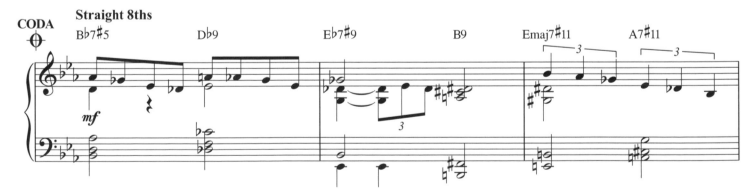

MEETING OF THE SPIRITS

By JOHN McLAUGHLIN

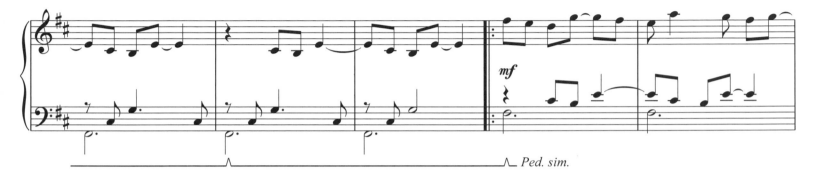

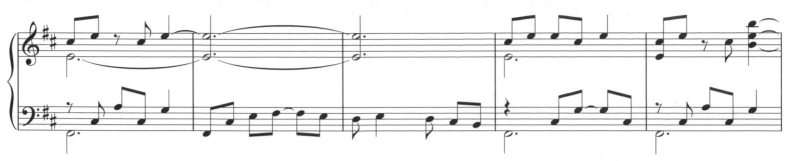

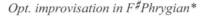

*Opt. improvisation in F#Phrygian**

* *The pitches of a D major scale from F# to F#.*

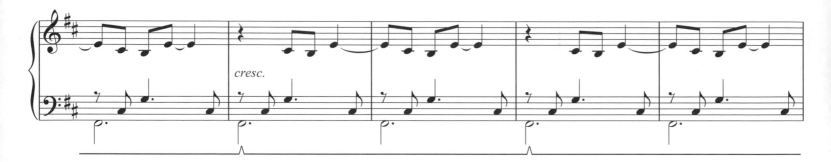

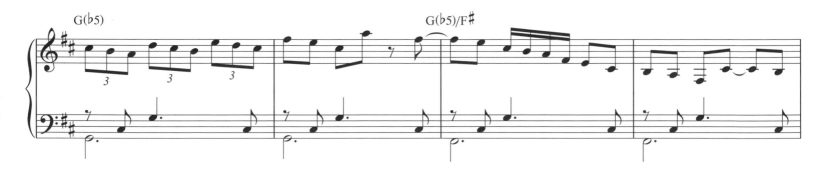

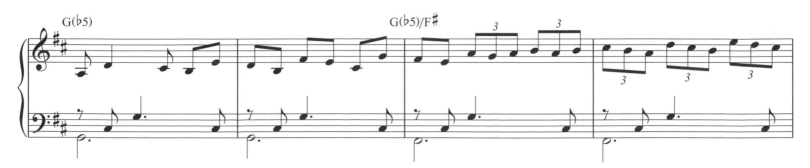

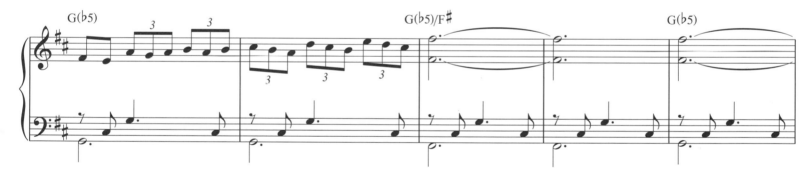

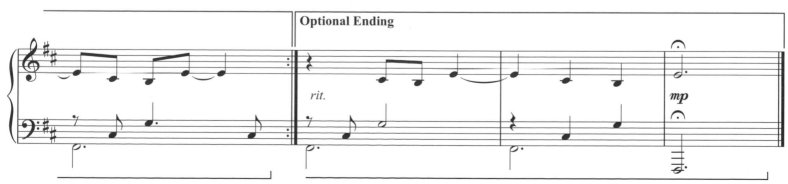

GOT A MATCH?

By CHICK COREA

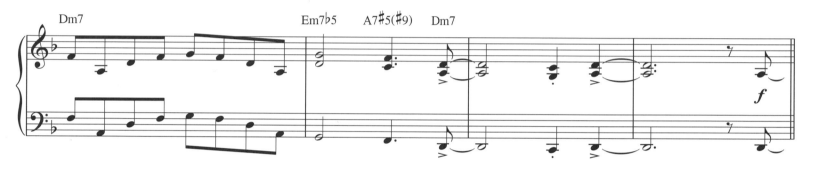

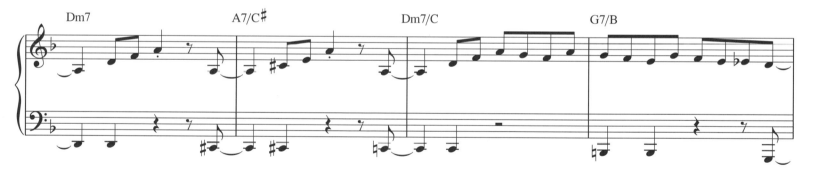

48

Solo based on one by Chick Corea

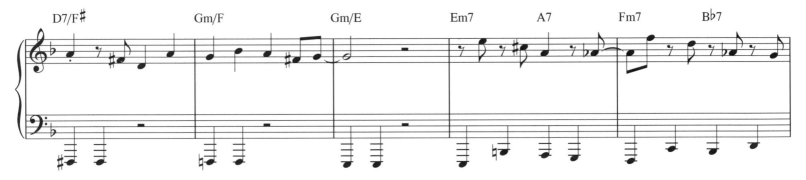

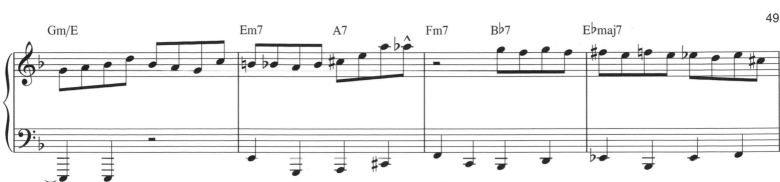

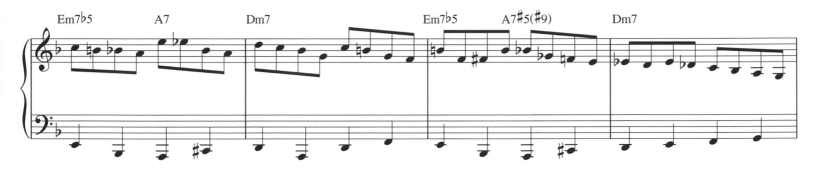

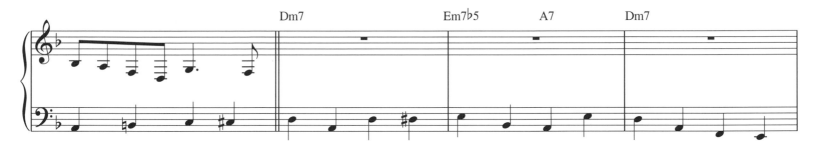

MERCY, MERCY, MERCY

By JOSEF ZAWINUL

Freely and soulfully

Moderate Gospel

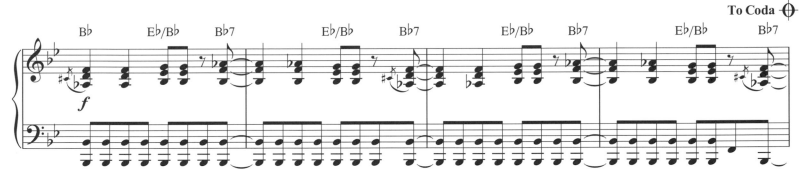

Solo based on one by Joe Zawinul

To Coda ⊕

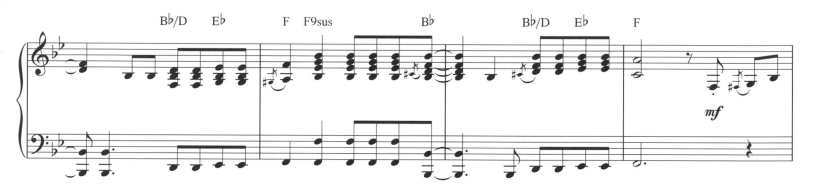

MILE HIGH

By RUSSELL FERRANTE, BILL GABLE,
JAMES HASLIP, WILLIAM KENNEDY
and MARC RUSSO

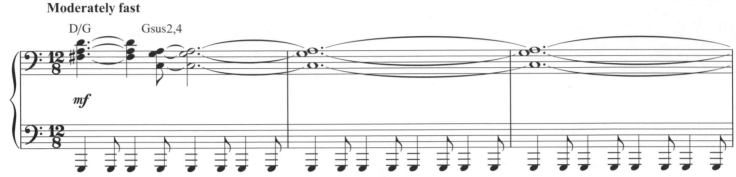

55

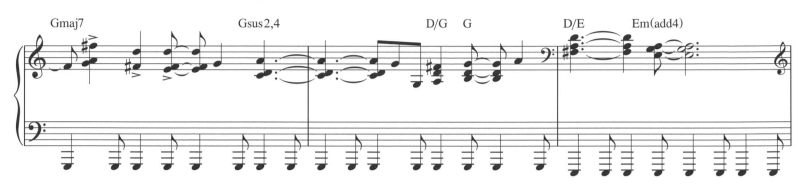

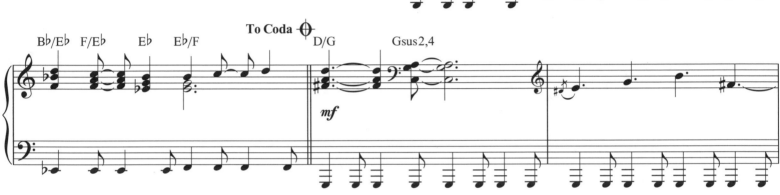

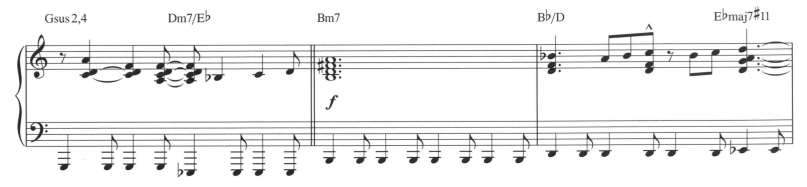

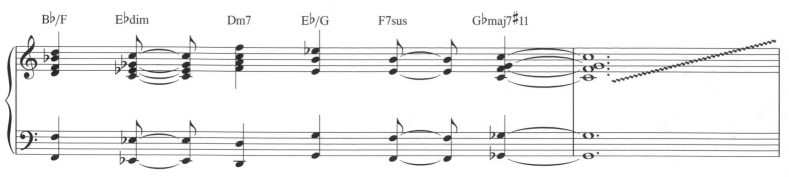

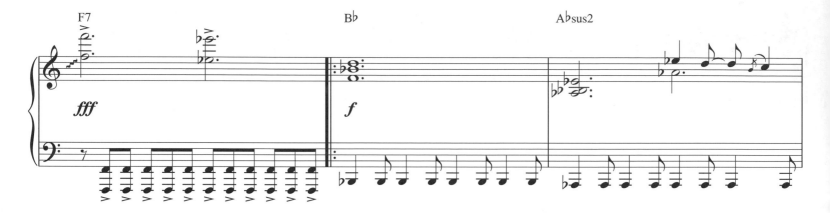

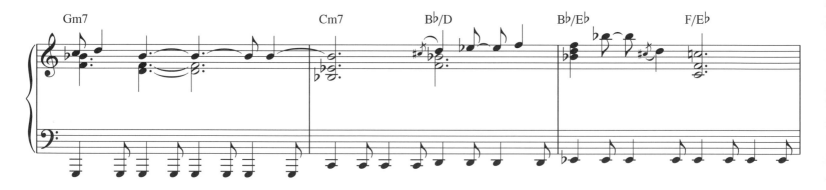

SNAKES

By MARCUS MILLER

Moderately fast

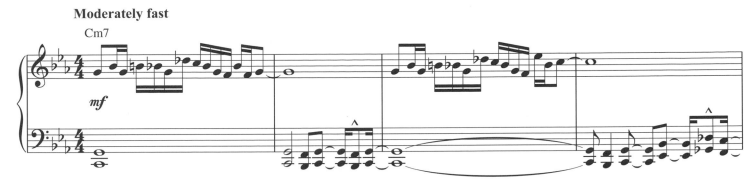

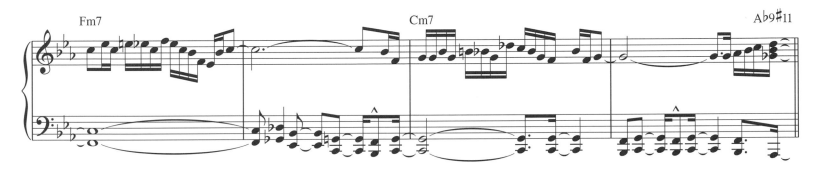

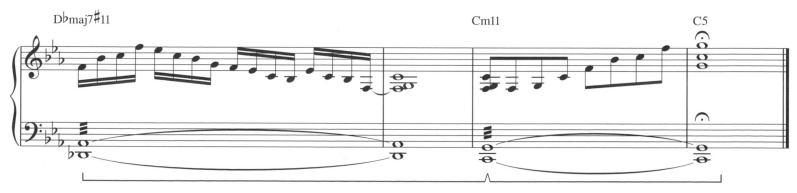

OOPS

By MIKE MAINIERI

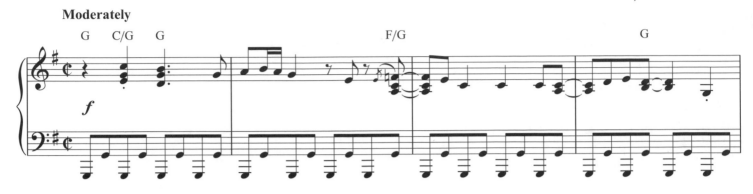

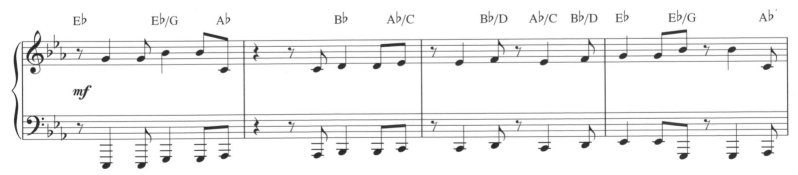

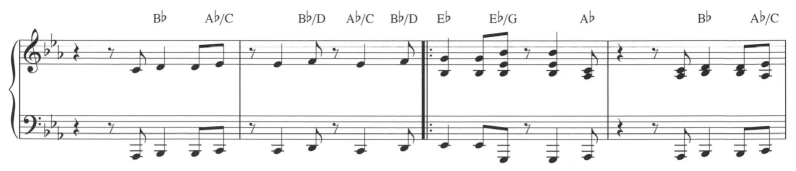

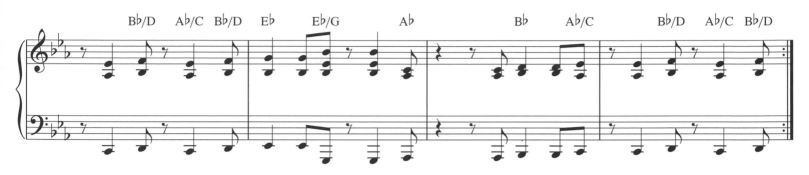

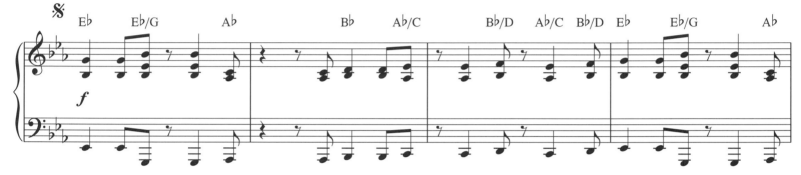

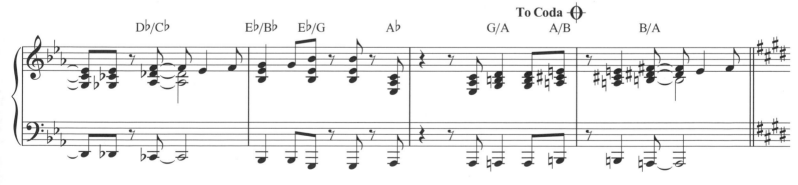

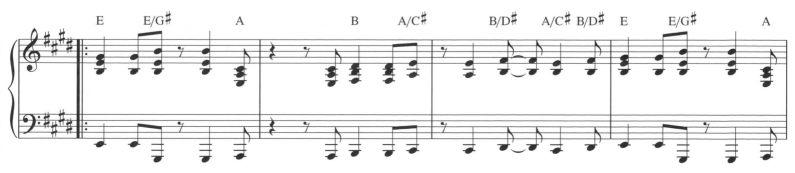

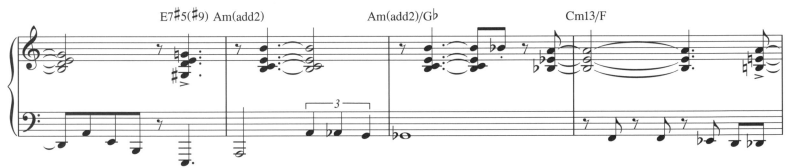

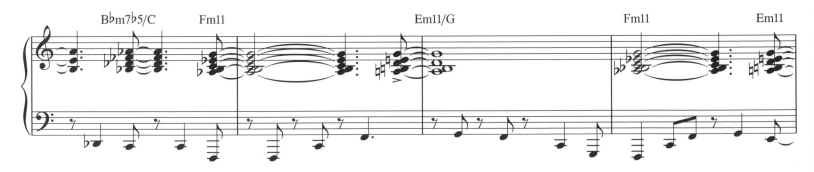

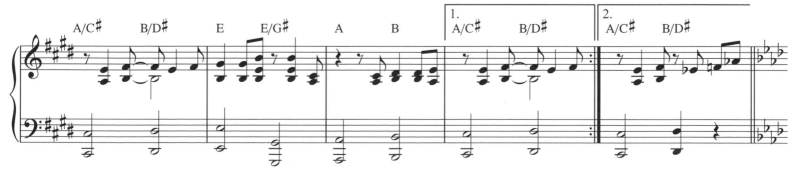

PEACHES EN REGALIA

By FRANK ZAPPA

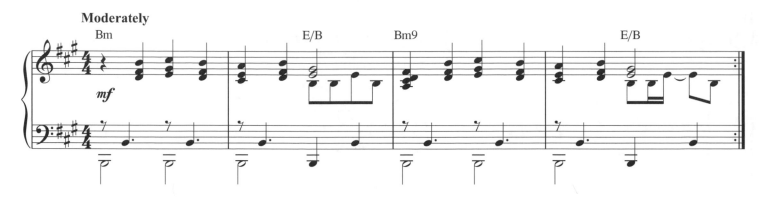

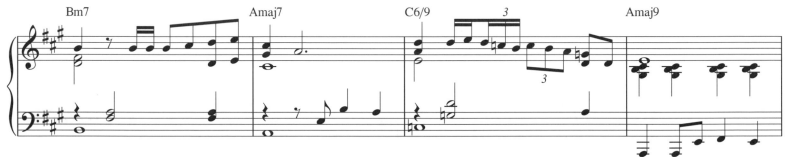

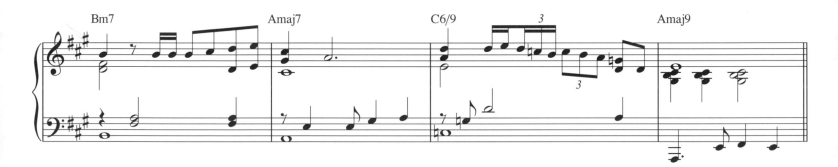

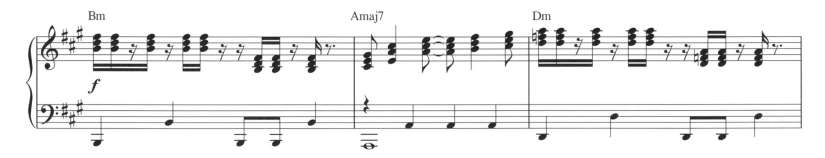

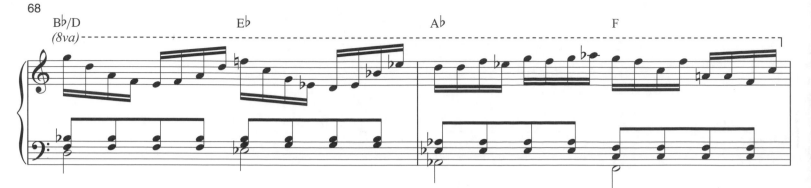

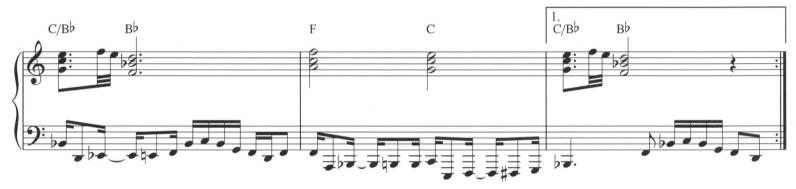

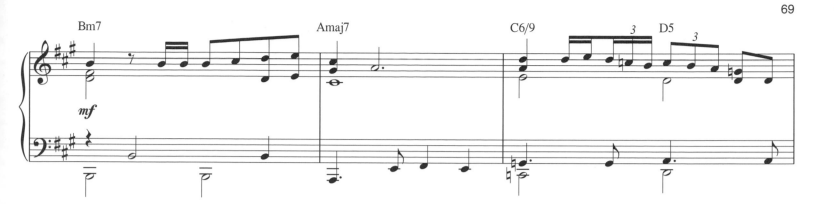

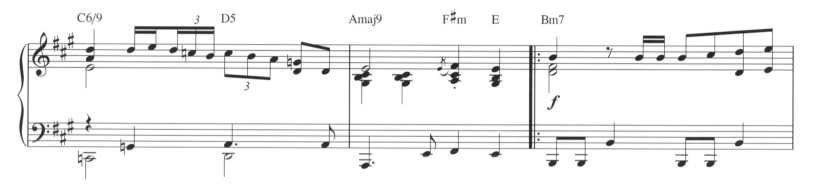

PORTRAIT OF TRACY

By JACO PASTORIUS

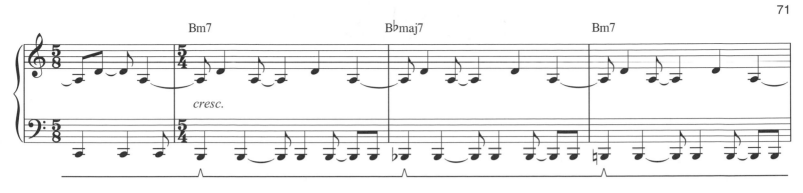

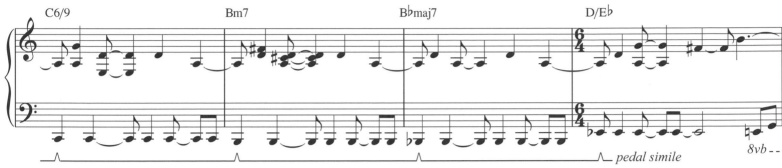

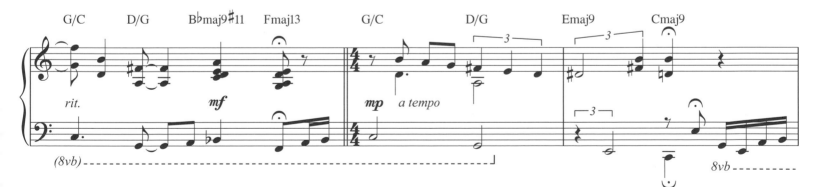

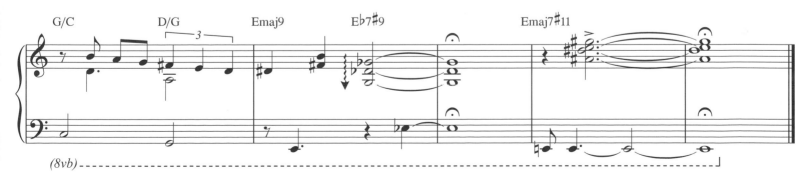

RED BARON

By BILLY COBHAM

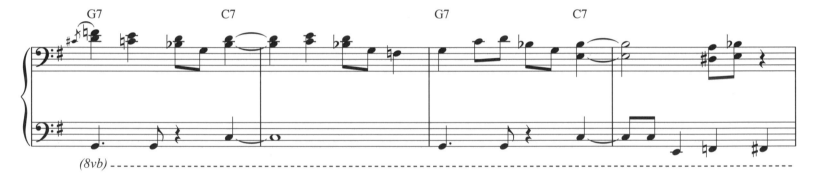

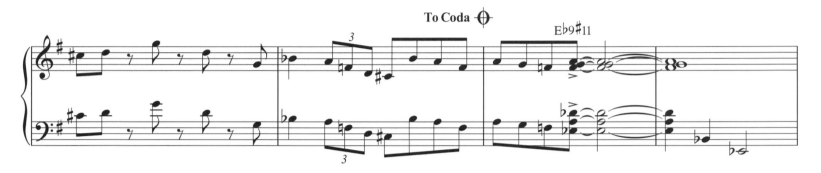

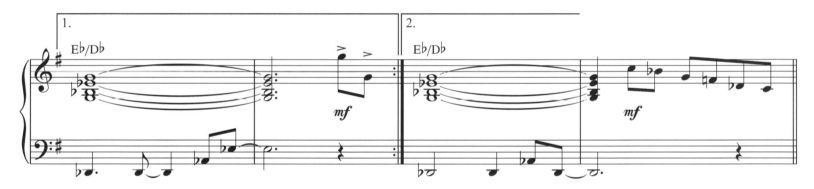

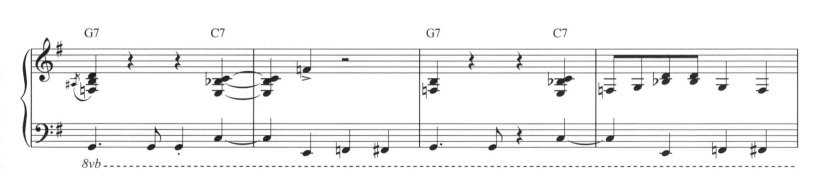

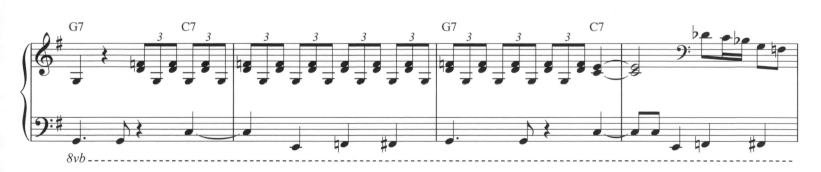

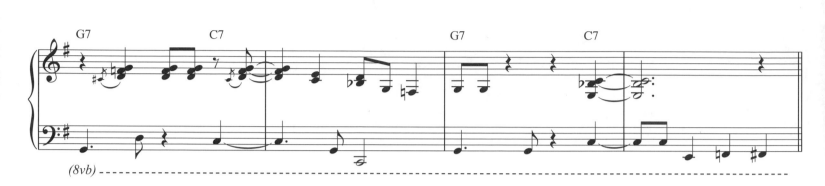

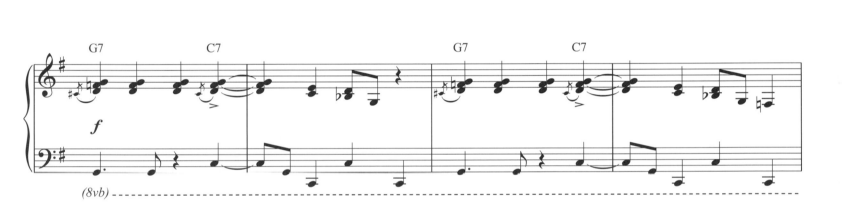

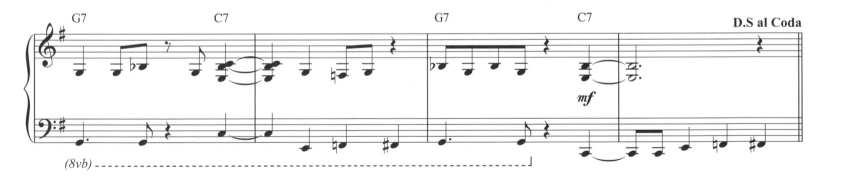

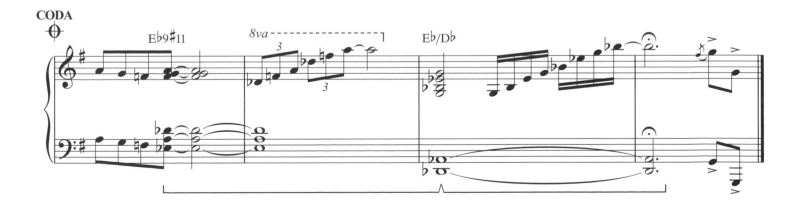

RED CLAY

By FREDDIE HUBBARD

Free time

Medium Rock groove

78

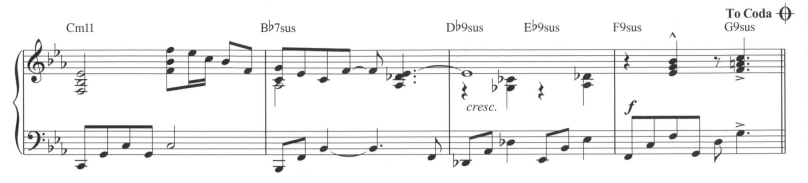

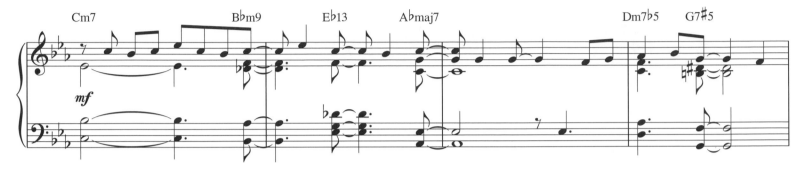

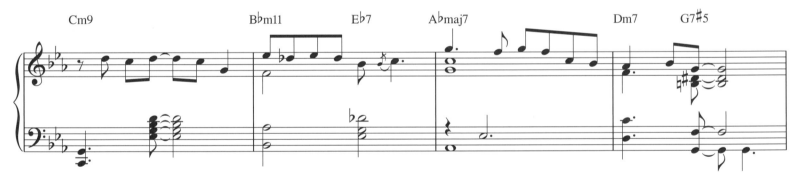

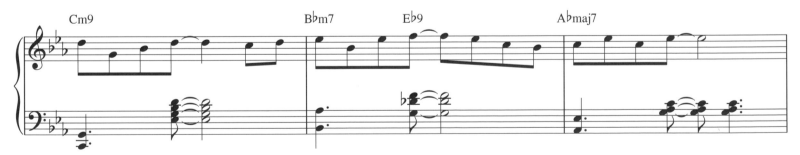

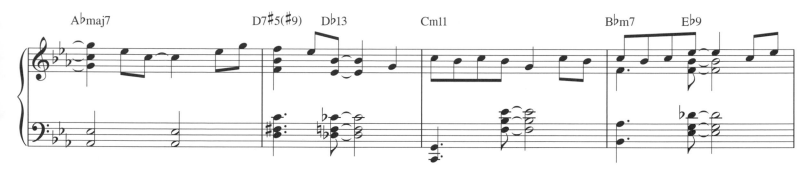

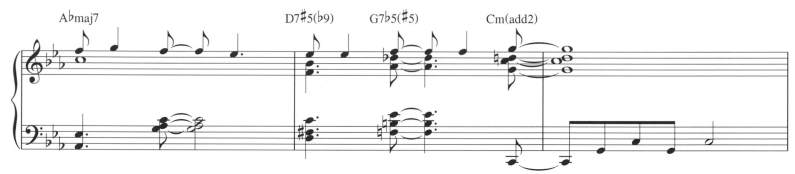

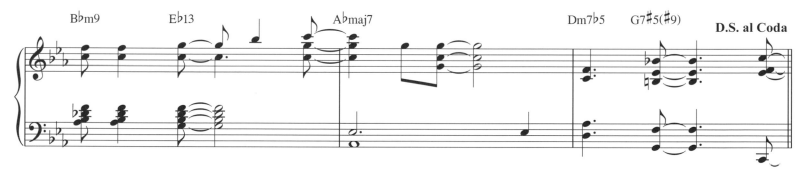

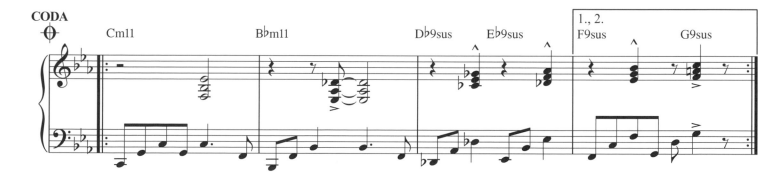

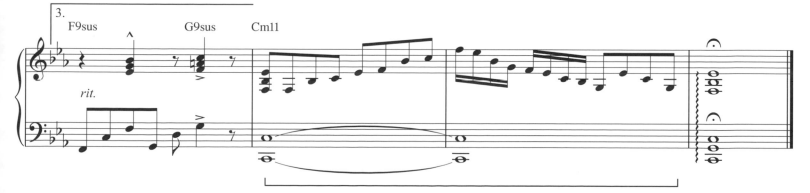

A REMARK YOU MADE

By JOSEF ZAWINUL

Ballad

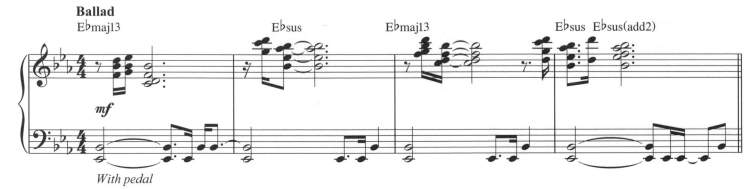

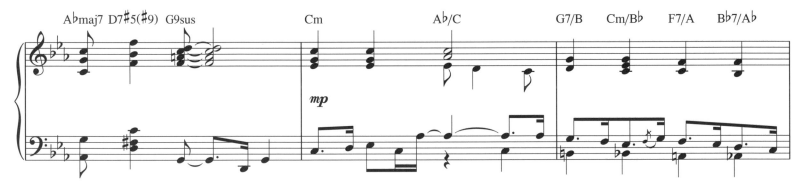

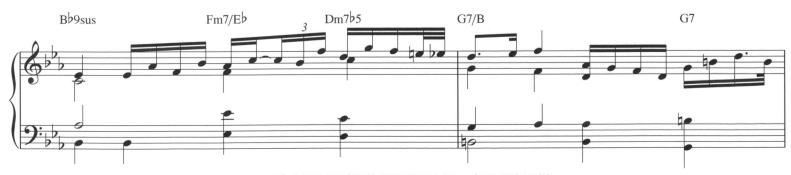

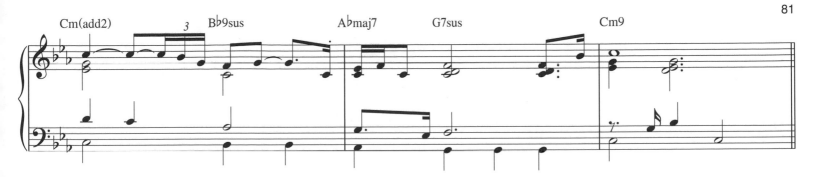

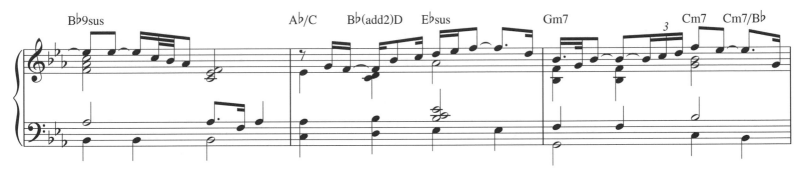

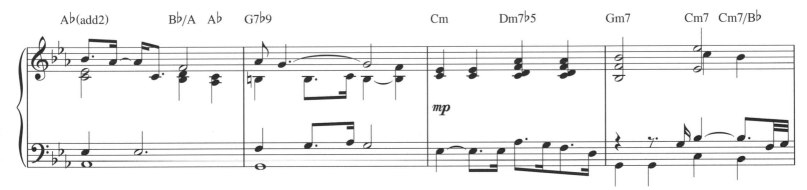

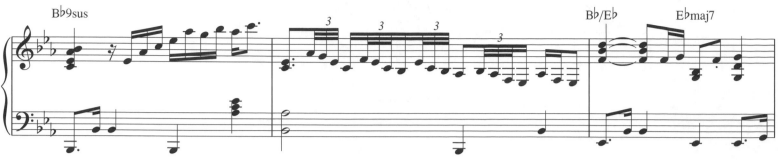

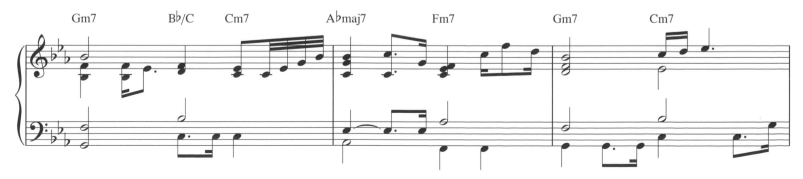

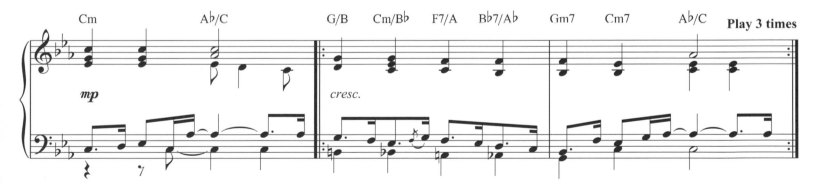

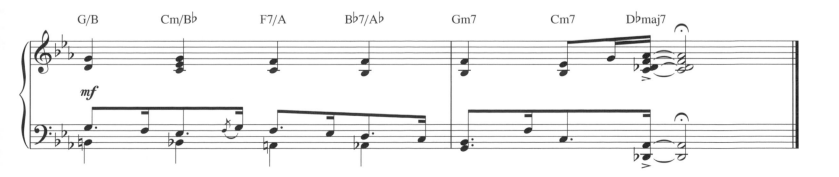

THING OF GOLD

By MICHAEL LEAGUE

Moderately

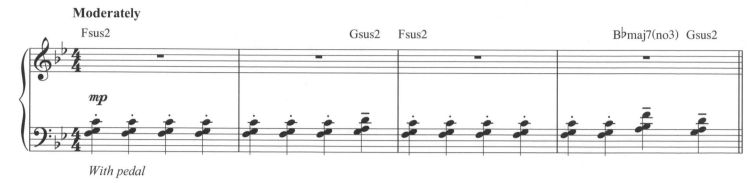

With pedal

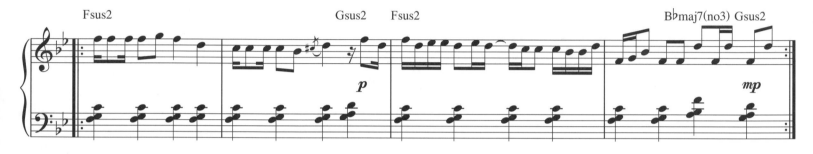

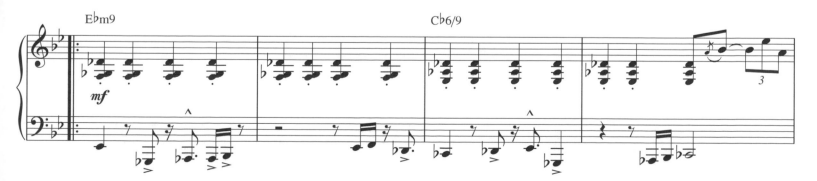

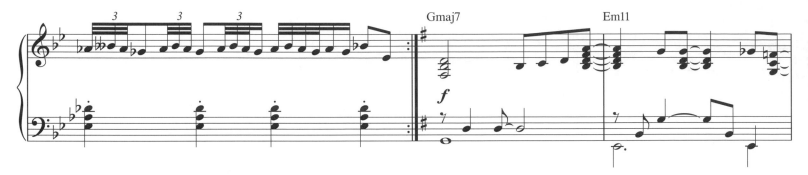

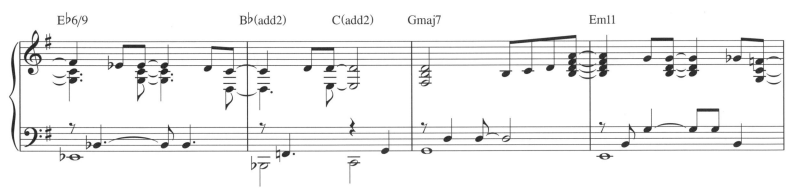

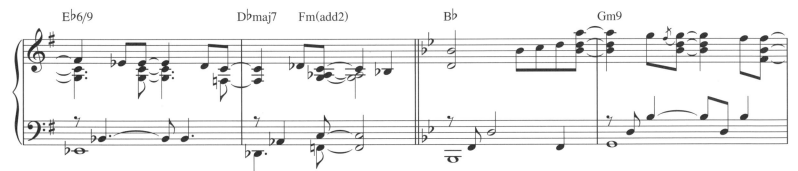

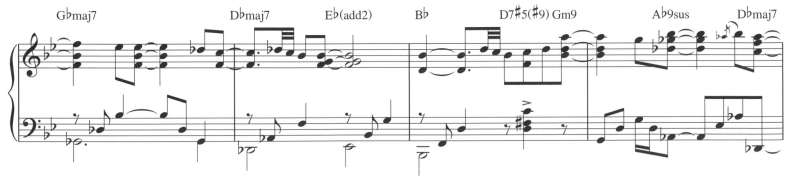

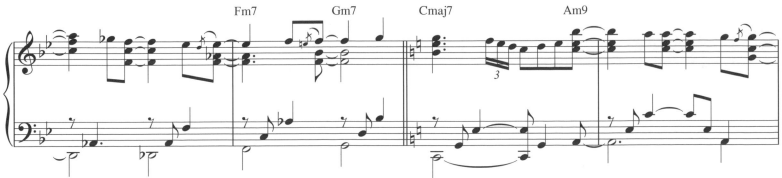

WINELIGHT

Words and Music by
WILLIAM EATON

Bright Swing

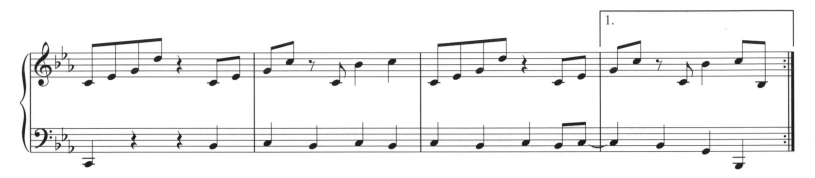

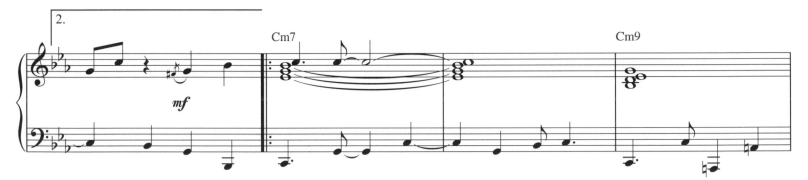

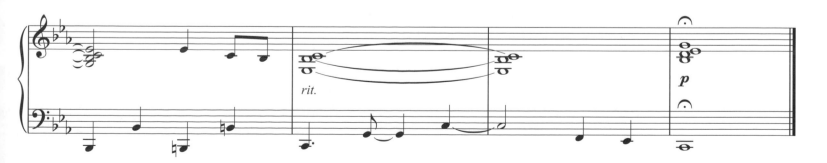

YOU KNOW WHAT I MEAN

By JEFF BECK
and MAX MIDDLETON

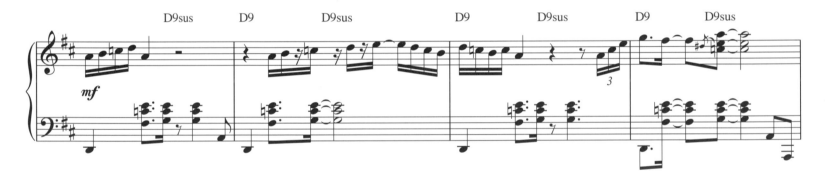

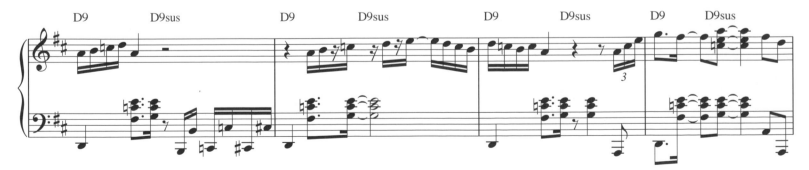

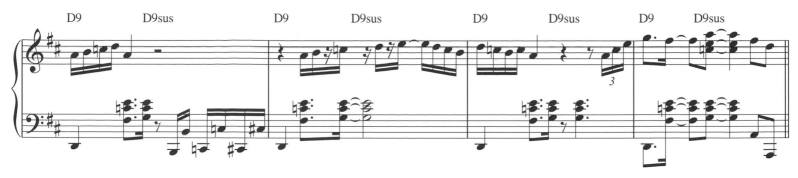

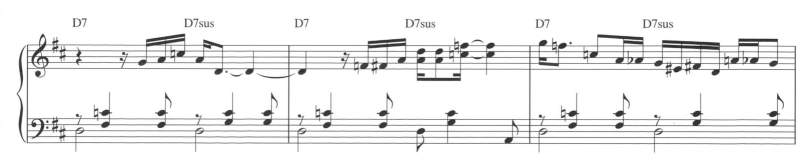

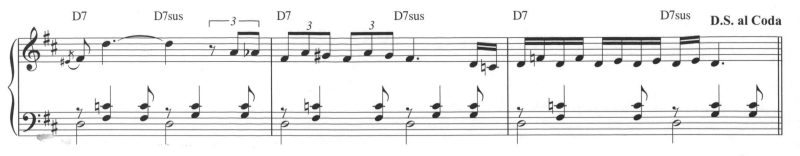

CODA

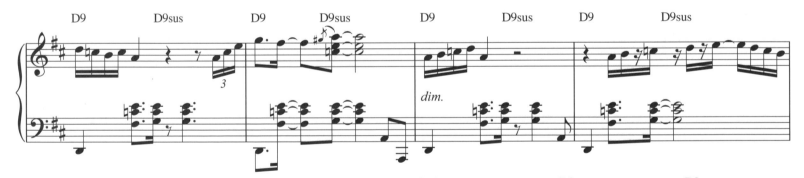

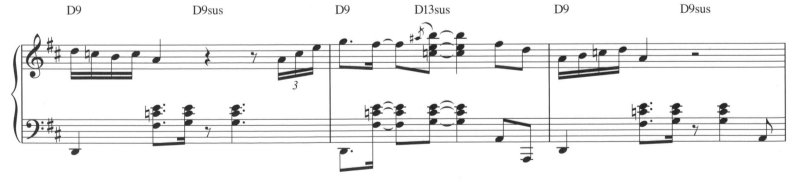

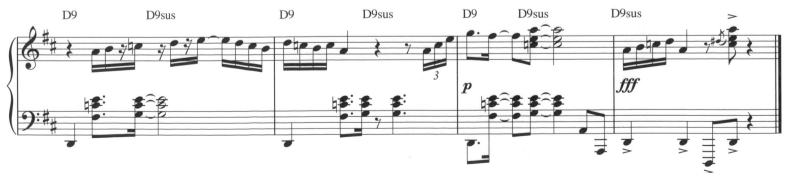